LEUKAEMIA

LEUKAEMIA LEUKAEMIA LEUKAEMIA LEUKAEMIA LEUKAEMIA LEUKAEMIA LEUKAEMIA LEUKAEMIA LEUKAEMIA LEUKAEMIA LEUKAEMIA LEUKAEMIA LEUKAEMIA LEUKAEMIA

A Parent's Guide

Priya Shah

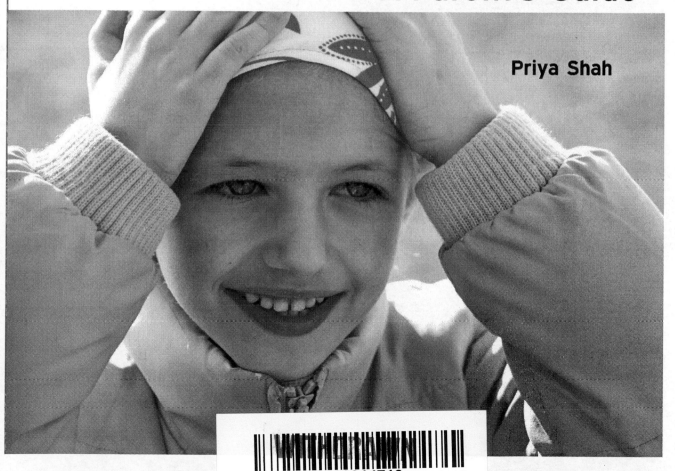

Leukaemia: The Essential Guide is also available in accessible formats for people with any degree of visual impairment. The large print edition and e-book (with accessibility features enabled) are available from Need2Know. Please let us know if there are any special features you require and we will do our best to accommodate your needs.

First published in Great Britain in 2012 by
Need2Know
Remus House
Coltsfoot Drive
Peterborough
PE2 9BF
Telephone 01733 898103
Fax 01733 313524
www.need2knowbooks.co.uk

Introduction

For any parent, a diagnosis of leukaemia in their child can evoke a huge range of emotions; from disbelief to denial, swiftly followed by devastation, shock, anger and an overriding sense of fear at the thought they could lose their loved one. There could be a sense of numbness, and perhaps hardest of all to bear: guilt. Did I miss the signs and symptoms? Could I have done something sooner? Such questions plague the minds of parents trying to come to terms with the news. These are all perfectly normal and understandable reactions in such a difficult situation, but with enough time and information, and a great deal of support and guidance, shock and uncertainty is replaced by the reality of what's happening and what you must do next.

After the initial shock of the diagnosis subsides, you may be left with what feels like an endless list of questions about the impact the illness will have on everyone and everything. Your first will probably be 'what does this mean for my child?' followed by 'what treatment do they need and how will it affect them?', 'how do we tell people?' and, 'if I have to leave work to be with my child throughout treatment, how will we cope financially?' All these concerns and more are addressed practically and sensitively in this guide.

It's important to understand that leukaemia not only affects children, a misconception some adults have, and that no one is ever completely safe from developing the condition. This is highlighted in the beginning of the book where the disease itself is explained, along with the signs and symptoms, and the different forms of leukaemia and who they can affect.

It discusses at length the necessary tests and procedures performed to obtain a diagnosis, detailing how a diagnosis is confirmed and what to expect next. The various treatments designed to treat leukaemia are described, plus their associated side effects and how you can best support your child through the physically demanding and emotionally draining treatment process.

There are chapters dedicated to coping techniques and support strategies, useful advice about relieving the financial burden is given, along with insights into dealing with the other effects on family life a diagnosis of leukaemia can bring. *Leukaemia: A Parent's Guide* finishes by providing a comprehensive list of resources and organisations you can access for further advice and support on your child's condition and any issues related to it.

Written primarily for parents whose son or daughter has received the devastating diagnosis of leukaemia, this informative guide offers support and guidance throughout every step of the emotionally challenging journey the disease takes them, their child and the rest of their family on.

Disclaimer

Please remember that the information provided in this book is not meant to replace the advice of a doctor or any other specialist, and you should always consult a healthcare professional in the first instance regarding any medical issues featured in this book or associated with the condition.

Chapter One

Leukaemia and Diagnosis: An Overview

What is leukaemia?

Leukaemia is a cancer of the blood and bone marrow. It affects certain blood cells, in particular white cells (leukocytes) which form part of the body's defence against infection and disease. Leukaemia is believed to start from one abnormal cell. It is thought that certain vital genes which control how cells divide, multiply and then die, are damaged or altered, resulting in an abnormal cell. If this abnormal cell survives, it then multiplies out of control, developing into leukaemia.

Leukaemia can strike anyone at any age; in the UK it is the most common form of childhood cancer, the ninth most common cancer in men and the 11th most common cancer in women.

Despite persistent and ongoing research, the causes of leukaemia have not yet been established.

'Leukaemia is a cancer of the blood and bone marrow.'

Childhood leukaemias – the statistics

The different forms of leukaemia that affect children, and their rates of incidence are as follows:

- Acute lymphoblastic leukaemia (ALL) – The most commonly occuring type, accounting for up to 70-80% of cases in children.

- Acute myeloid leukaemia (AML) – The next most common, seen in around 20% of diagnoses.

- Chronic myeloid leukaemia (CML) – About 50% of leukaemia diagnoses are of this type.
- The remaining percentages are a combination of unusual and rare forms of childhood leukaemia.

The different types of leukaemia that affect both adults and children will be discussed in more detail in the following section.

Depending on which form of the disease your child has makes a difference in the initial symptoms and subsequent treatment. Knowing all that you can about your child's leukaemia can help you to explain the disease to loved ones and to make sure that they understand what is going on every step of the way.

Different forms of leukaemia

Leukaemia can come in several different forms with differing severities and outcomes. Some may not affect children, or will rarely affect children. Once you have a diagnosis, then you can ask for more information from your healthcare team, and conduct your own research.

'Leukaemia is first classified as either acute or chronic.'

Leukaemia is first classified as either acute or chronic.

- Acute – This means the disease develops and progresses quite quickly. Acute leukaemia is the rapid increase of immature blood cells. The increased blood cells make it impossible for the bone marrow to produce healthy blood cells. Immediate treatment is needed for this type of leukaemia due to the rapid progression of this disease. Unfortunately, this is one of the most common types that affects children. If caught early there may be a better chance of successful treatment.

- Chronic – Means the disease develops and progresses slowly (even without treatment). Chronic leukaemia is the build-up of white blood cells. These white blood cells will be abnormal. The progression of this particular leukaemia is extremely slow with it taking months, even years, to progress. In some cases this type of leukaemia will be watched and studied before taking action to make sure that the right action is taken. This type of leukaemia is generally seen in older individuals but can be seen in children. With children, this disease is usually slow progressing and can be successfully treated, with great recovery rates.

The main types of leukaemia are:

- Acute lymphoblastic leukaemia (ALL) – This form of leukaemia is the most common to affect children. It can affect adults but typically those who are over the age of 65. Chemotherapy and radiation are typical treatments with survival rates being 85% in children.

- Chronic lymphocytic leukaemia (CLL) – This particular form of leukaemia typically affects adults over the age of 60 but can sometimes occur in teenage children. There have been a few isolated cases of young children having this form. The survival rate is 75% in five years. It is incurable but can be managed with effective treatments.

- Acute myeloid leukaemia (AML) – This leukaemia is rare in children and tends to occur more commonly in adults over 50. The survival rate is 40% and it is treated with chemotherapy.

- Chronic myeloid leukaemia (CML) – The rarest form, this disease has occurred in some children but mostly attacks adults becoming more common with increasing age. The survival rate for this leukaemia is at 90% at five years.

Some particulary rare forms of leukaemia include:

- Hairy cell leukaemia – There are no known cases of this type of leukaemia in children. This disease typically affects people aged 40-60, particularly men, and is highly treatable with a 96% survival rate.

- T-cell prolymphocytic leukaemia – A very rare leukaemia that has a survival rate of just a few months in typical cases. This form is extremely aggressive, primarily affecting adults over the age of 30.

A note about survival rates

Many times there are estimates about the length of time that someone with a leukaemia diagnosis will live. This is called a survival rate. It is based on the age of your child, the progression of the disease and the type of leukaemia. The rate is usually given as a five-year rate because this is considered a positive and encouraging amount of time to be free of the cancer and any studies of patients who have survived leukaemia or other cancers may be easily tracked through the five-year mark.

Knowledge is power

Knowledge of this disease is the best weapon that you can have. Do your research and make sure that you find out as much reliable information as you can about leukaemia so that you can be up to date on everything that happens with your child. Be proactive in your child's healthcare and make sure that you ask all the questions you can think of and ask the doctor for further information and access to research studies completed on the particular type of leukaemia your child is diagnosed with.

Here are some questions to ask the doctor after a leukaemia diagnosis:

'Knowledge of this disease is the best weapon that you can have.'

- What is the type of leukaemia that my child has?
- What is the correct spelling?
- What are the next steps?
- Will my child experience much pain associated with treatment?
- What are the treatment options?
- Will my child be hospitalised for a long time?
- What side effects can be expected?
- What is the prognosis or expected survival rate for this type of leukaemia?
- Do you have any information or suggestions about talking to my child about the illness?
- Who can I talk to about financial resources?

- Are there other doctors for a second opinion?

- Who will be on the treatment team?

- How soon does treatment start?

- Do you have any suggestions of housing or accommodations should the hospital be too far away from home to get to easily?

- Can you get some information about support groups and counselling for my child and our family?

Leukaemia signs and symptoms

As we know, leukaemia is a cancer of blood-forming cells, and when the abnormal cells are produced they spill out into the bloodstream producing a number of symptoms including:

- Anaemia – As the number of red blood cells decreases, anaemia develops causing tiredness and breathlessness, amongst other symptoms. The complexion becomes noticeably paler as well.

- Blood clotting problems – Resulting from the low levels of platelets in the bloodstream, causing bleeding gums, easy bruising and other bleeding-related issues.

- Serious infections – Resulting from the reduced number of white blood cells that normally fight infection. Symptoms of infections can vary greatly, depending on the type and where they are located.

These symptoms can present themselves differently, depending on which form of leukaemia the patient is suffering from. In the cases of ALL or AML, symptoms can typically develop within weeks, however it can take months or even years to display the symptoms for CLL or CML, as these are the slow-progressing variations of the disease.

Other signs of the illness include:

- Swollen glands in various parts of the body

- Joint and bone pain (mainly associated with ALL)

- Persistent fever

* Weight loss

Symptoms of childhood leukaemia

Signs and symptoms of leukaemia can often mirror those of a common viral illness, a cold or the flu; making it difficult to identify the disease initially and delaying prompt diagnosis and treatment.

Common symptoms include:

* General fatigue, lethargy and malaise
* Shortness of breath and/or reduced exercise ability
* Bone and muscle pain (particularly in the legs)
* Recurrent or prolonged fevers and common childhood infections
* Irritability
* Bleeding gums and/or bruising easily
* Prolonged/troublesome cough
* Headache
* Nausea/vomiting
* Dizziness and palpitations
* Failure to thrive and growth retardation

Diagnosis

Leukaemia is usually diagnosed and assessed by the following:

* A blood test – This detects any abnormal cells present in the blood which suggest leukaemia. If leukaemia is suspected, further tests are carried out to confirm the diagnosis.
* A bone marrow sample – This is not always necessary for diagnosis, but if samples are collected they are examined under a microscope to look for abnormal cells as well as tested in other ways. Bone marrow samples are collected by inserting a needle into the pelvic bone or breastbone.

- Lumbar puncture – A small amount of cerebrospinal fluid (CSF) is collected from around the spinal cord by inserting a needle between the vertebrae at the bottom of the patient's back. The fluid is examined for leukaemia cells and to assess if the disease has spread.

- Cell and chromosome analysis – Any abnormal cells found in any of the above tests undergo more detailed examinations to determine the exact type or subtype of the cell that is abnormal.

The diagnosis of your child's condition will come after the doctors have had time to examine the blood tests and any other tests that have been done. Your doctor will be able to tell you if leukaemia has been diagnosed, and if so, what form your child has as well as the prognosis of your child's condition. Leukaemia can, at times, be hard to diagnosis. You may have to go through many different doctors to get the diagnosis. Some versions may hide and not be easily detected, so this is why you may have to go through many different tests and see a variety of doctors.

Prognosis

Some childhood leukaemias can be easily treated if caught early enough. The prognosis (outlook) is often good for those who suffer from a chronic form of leukaemia as it is a very slow-progressing disease. Those who suffer from an acute form of leukaemia may have a less favourable prognosis depending on several factors. The first being how long the patient has had the disease and if it has spread to any other organs. From there factors such as how the patient will respond to the varied treatments will all increase or decrease the prognosis for the future.

The general outlook

The prognosis for each different form of leukaemia varies, however the general outlook is better than most people imagine. Treatments are progressing and survival rates are increasing all the time. For example, the outlook for ALL has improved tremendously over the last 20 years or so. Happily, most children that are diagnosed with ALL (about 7-8 in 10 cases) can be cured. For those suffering from a chronic form (CLL and CML) which are not cured, effective treatments can often prolong survival for quite some time.

Treatment options will depend on what type of leukaemia your child is diagnosed with. The most common forms of treatment are chemotherapy and radiation. These treatment options are hard on your child but necessary to help vanquish the disease. In some cases, for milder forms of leukaemia, other medications may be given. It is not recommended to give your child any holistic medicines during the battle with leukaemia as they can have an adverse reaction to the chemotherapy or radiation. Simple but important ways to help treatment is by making sure that your child stays hydrated and eats a good meal when they can. You will have to make sure that you monitor your child every day for symptoms related to the chemotherapy and radiation, and watch for any other symptoms from the leukaemia itself. Keeping an eye on your child and their symptoms will help the doctors with their treatment plans.

'The prognosis for each different form of leukaemia varies, however the general outlook is better than most people imagine.'

Summing Up

- Leukaemia is a cancer of the blood and bone marrow.

- Leukaemia is first classified as either acute or chronic.

- The four main types of leukaemia are: acute lymphoblastic leukaemia (ALL), chronic lymphocytic leukaemia (CLL), acute myeloid leukaemia (AML) and chronic myeloid leukaemia (CML).

- ALL is the most common form of leukaemia to affect children.

- Blood tests, bone marrow tests and lumbar puncture are among the tests carried out to determine diagnosis.

- Prognosis for different forms varies, but is often not as bleak as expected, with cure rates in some types increasing greatly.

Chapter Two

Diagnosis – What Now?

Hearing that your child has leukaemia can be one of the most frightening and devasting things as a parent you ever hear in your life. Leukaemia can be a long, hard road for a child and their family. There are many things that you will want to consider.

Telling your child

One of the most common questions and dilemmas parents face is whether or not to tell the child that they are sick. For younger children it will be hard to explain and they may not understand. For older children it may be upsetting and hard for them to understand why it is happening to them. If you do decide to tell your child that they are facing leukaemia it is imperative that you have a support system around them so that they know they have support and love during this challenging time. Always make sure that you speak to your child's doctor about telling your child about their illness and get their opinion and advice. You may want to enlist the doctor's assistance when the time comes to help answer some of your child's questions.

'Always make sure that you speak to your child's doctor about telling your child about their illness and get their opinion and advice.'

Moving/Temporary relocation

It may seem a drastic decision and quite an upheaval, but another thing to consider would be moving closer to the hospital providing treatment. Treatment for childhood leukaemia is carried out in specialist centres/hospitals, meaning that once diagnosed, your child could be transferred to a treatment centre many miles from where you live. Treatment for the disease involves prolonged periods of time in hospital, often several months, and this can only add to the already tremendous strain on the family. You will have to attend many different appointments and treatments, and may benefit from having less driving time to get to and from these. Many parents find that they have to drive hours from their home, especially if they live in a rural area. With petrol prices being at an all time high (at the time of writing) you will have to determine what to do as far as living arrangements are concerned. For some families, renting a property near to where treatment is taking place is the answer. However, this is not financially viable for many families. Fortunately, there are some amazing charities that provide much needed accommodation to families with sick children, helping to ease the difficulty and pain of being away from home, whilst offering invaluable support through the child's illness. One such organisation is The Sick Children's Trust. They run eight 'houses' near key treatment facilities, such as Addenbrooke's Hospital in Cambridge, that consist of up to 15 family bedrooms, 9 bathrooms, communal dining areas for socialising and well-stocked playrooms to cater for siblings. Find out more about the fantastic work they do at www.sickchildrenstrust.org or see the help list for further contact details.

Taking time off work

Following on from accommodation, the next obvious consideration is about taking time off of work during your child's treatment. You may be going to the doctor, hospital or treatment facility several times during the week, so staying in your job may not be an option. Most companies will allow you to take time off work during your child's treatment if you tell them what is happening. Be sure to talk to your boss if your child has been diagnosed with leukaemia and see what you can do about a compromise with your work and being there for your child. If the situation means one parent is forced to give up work completely, you should investigate what benefits may be available to you. The loss of one income will obviously affect the entire family's financial wellbeing and add to the existing huge burden of worry. For more details on this see chapter 4 and the help list.

School

Being diagnosed with leukaemia means your child may not be able to go to school for some time, so you may want to consider an alternative method of schooling (such as a private tutor) for when they reach a certain point in their recovery and are able to return to studies. With leukaemia the immune system will be severely compromised and a cold can quickly turn into a life-threatening infection, so you will have to take extreme caution when the time comes for your child to return to school. Talk with your doctor about what would be best for your child.

After you have the doctor's recommendations and have a better idea of the treatment schedule, you can speak to your child's teacher(s) and to the school to adapt schoolwork. Your child's classmates and friends will also need to know some information since your child will be absent for some time and some physical changes like hair loss will be obvious to them. You can decide how much information is shared with people outside of your home, but make sure that they have enough so that they can be supportive and respectful of the process that you and your family are going through.

Support through tests and treatment

Tests such as bone marrow tests, and lumbar punctures can cause considerable discomfort and pain, so you will have to decide whether or not you want to be present for some or all of these things. Every parent wants to be with their child while they are undergoing treatments and procedures to provide comfort and support, but some find it extremely hard to witness them going through such pain, and find that difficulty coping with their own emotions makes it hard to be a source of reassurance and comfort the child needs. In this instance the harsh reality may be that it is better for the parent not to be present during procedures as the child will benefit more positively from the attention of the specially trained professionals. This is why it is important that you are accurately informed about exactly what will happen every step of the way. To be a good support for your child you don't want to be in the middle of a procedure and have to leave, so you must know your own limits.

You will also want to consider the side effects of the treatment and the long-term effects on your child. Most treatments can cause many different side effects including nausea, joint pain, hair loss, vomiting, stomach trouble, headaches and many other symptoms. Chemotherapy and radiotherapy can be extremely hard to go through for anyone no matter the age, so you will have

'The harsh reality may be that it is better for the parent not to be present during procedures as the child will benefit more positively from the attention of the specially trained professionals.'

to make sure that you are ready to give comfort and support whenever your child might need it. You can read more about side effects from treatment in chapter 3.

Helping your child cope

Easing your child's mind about the disease is something else that you may want to consider. A child, depending on their age, will know something is wrong by the way they feel, and as the adults in their world find out about the diagnosis they may behave differently, alerting the child that something is wrong.

A younger child, 0-2 years, will not know much, but it is very important for you to make sure that you ease their fears and help to comfort them. A trip to the playroom at the hospital and other fun things will help make everything easier.

An older child, 3-10 years, may be very aware of what is going on and develop stress and anxiety issues. Things like games, movies, playrooms, and as many things that you can do to keep their mind off what is going on is extremely helpful and important.

Children in the preteen and teenage years will require attention from you and others to help them accept their diagnosis and fight the disease. Friends at this age are very important and so helping your child to maintain connections during treatment may help a great deal. Computers and a mobile phone to help them stay in contact and in touch with what is going on socially may help your teen with some of the stress and anxiety they experience.

You will also need to consider ways to increase your child's self-esteem, should they need it. Often, hair loss will be a result of treatment, so you may have to help your child decide if they want to wear a wig, or help them pick out some head scarves that suit their taste. Many children are very upset at the loss of their hair, girls more so than boys. Making sure that you have a support system for your child can ensure that your child's self-esteem is kept as high as possible.

Helping your child to be at ease with as much of the treatment as possible will be an ongoing process, with some fears surfacing at different times. It is important to keep the lines of communication open and to continue to support them whatever their feelings.

Love

Your child is going to need lots and lots of love during this time from you and their family. Make sure that you tell your child how much you love them and make sure you do as much as you can to show them that. If your child has siblings ensure that you also convey your affection toward them, as well. This way you can make it a family mantra to voice your feelings about each other. The other children will understand just how important they are to you too, helping to avoid jealousy issues arising at an already difficult time. Since the ill child will have more attention because of their circumstances, you want to make sure the others are also cared for during this time. Affection in the form of hugs and kisses is very important during this time, for your child(ren) and for yourself and your partner.

Facing the ultimate fear

Even though you may not want to consider it you may have to face the possibililty of death at some point or another, and your child may question it. While some leukaemias are treatable, tragically, some are incurable, and you may have to approach this devastating and upsetting subject with your child. The support of family, friends and the doctors will help your child get through this. At some point you will have to make the decision whether or not you want to consider a hospice. A hospice will look after your child towards the end of their life, helping with everyday needs, providing care and comfort. The hospice will also help with after death care and making sure your child's wishes are fulfilled, but most importantly, they will make sure that your child is comfortable during their last days. While no parent ever wants to think about it, the help of a hospice may be something you will need to consider depending on the prognosis of your child's leukaemia.

Telling family and friends

One of the hardest things you will do after your child's diagnosis will be telling your family and friends about your child's diagnosis. While this is difficult to do it is always best to make sure that you inform your friends and family so that they can give you and your family support during this worrying time. For close family make sure that you tell them in person and that you let them know your child's prognosis and if they can do anything to help. Remember that they are you and your child's support system and will make sure you have the support and love that you'll need in the future. The diagnosis of leukaemia will affect the whole family and will make your home life tough, so ensuring that you are close to everyone in your home and in your family is very important. If your child has siblings sit down with them and explain what is going on and make sure that you offer them support and love as well.

'Telling people about the diagnosis can be overwhelming, but the support provided by loved ones cannot be overestimated.'

Also, remember that during initial conversations about the diagnosis and treatment, you will only be able to provide the details that you know yourself at that point; inevitably, questions and concerns will arise after the loved ones have thought about things for a while. Be prepared for these questions, that you may not have the answers to, and to perhaps have to go through it all again, explaining the diagnosis. Be sensitive as they process the information, as you expect them to be sensitive to you.

Depending on the age of the child and the siblings, you may want to decide how much information is given and at what time to share it with them. Also use language that the children will understand or explain terminology as needed. The explanation of some terms may be needed for your adult family members as well, depending on their understanding of the disease and medical treatments.

Telling people about the diagnosis can be overwhelming, but the support provided by loved ones cannot be overestimated.

Summing Up

- Following the diagnosis of leukaemia, many important factors affecting home life will need to be considered, such as moving house or relocating temporarily, perhaps leaving work, and schooling.

- You must be fully informed about the necessary tests and treatment your child will undergo, in order for you to provide the best support and reassurance possible during this frightening and uncertain time in their life.

- Emotionally, you must be prepared to consider how you will tell your child and then friends and family, and how you will put a support system in place to help you all cope.

Chapter Three

Tests and Treatments for Leukaemia

When your child does not feel well, there are symptoms that may give some clue as to what is wrong. Is there a loss of appetite, or fever? Or maybe your child is always tired or too worn out to play? Swollen lymph nodes or glands are also signs that the body is reacting to something. These symptoms help the doctor to decide what tests may be needed to pinpoint the problem. If leukaemia or other cancer is suspected, the most common types of tests used are biopsy, imaging tests, endoscopic tests, and laboratory tests. These give the doctor the information that is needed to provide the best treatment for your child.

We mentioned the different methods of testing for leukaemia in chapter 1, we will now look at them again in more detail.

Common tests

With any diagnosis, tests are performed to gather as much information as possible about your illness. The doctor may ask many questions about you, your immediate family and even your grandparents. This history of the family can point to health trends that make it more possible for you to have one illness or another.

During the initial consultation with your child the doctor will gather as much information as possible about your family's health and talk to you about how your child is feeling and what symptoms may be present. The doctor may then conduct a physical exam and may order blood tests.

'If leukaemia or other cancer is suspected, the most common types of tests used are biopsy, imaging tests, endoscopic tests, and laboratory tests.'

Blood is drawn, usually in a vein in the arm, and sent to a laboratory. The blood cells can be analysed in the laboratory and the number of platelets and red and white blood cells can be determined. If a very high level of white blood cells is present, then leukaemia may be a possible diagnosis. If leukaemia is suspected, further examination of the blood is carried out to determine a diagnosis.

In addition to counting and determining the health of the cells, the laboratory may also look for any abnormalities within the chromosomes of the cells. This is helpful in diagnosing the type of leukaemia because some, such as CML, have a specific abnormal chromosome in the cells.

A bone marrow biopsy or aspiration may be ordered. An aspiration is a way to remove fluid from somewhere. In this case the fluid is drawn from the bone. A biopsy is the removal of a bit of tissue; in this case a small piece of the bone. The tissue sample is sent to the lab to test it. Both the biopsy and aspiration are performed by inserting a hollow needle into a large bone, in the pelvis or sternum and removing some tissue/fluid. This can often be done in a single visit and with only some numbing of the area where the needle is inserted. This test may not be needed for a diagnosis of CLL.

Another test that involves the use of a needle is a lumbar puncture (sometimes called a spinal tap). This is done by inserting a needle in-between the vertebrae in the lower spine and removing some of the cerebrospinal fluid. This fluid fills the spinal cord and also surrounds the brain. This fluid sample is then tested to determine if leukaemia cells are present and also if the disease has spread to the spinal cord or brain, and the results are sent to your doctor.

Sometimes a chest X-ray is ordered because it may actually show swollen lymph nodes. It can be also done as a base-line test or one that gives a 'before' picture. That way, if for some reason there is an impact on your child's lungs or chest area, the first X-ray done prior to treatment can be compared with the later films to show any differences or changes.

Once the tests are completed, you will attend an appointment and speak with the doctor to discuss the results. He or she will share all the test results and make sure that you understand them. They will then tell you what the tests point to as far as a diagnosis.

Even though it may seem like a great deal of testing to go through for a diagnosis, the more information a doctor can gather, then the faster a diagnosis can be given, the better the treatment can be and the sooner it can begin.

Treatment options

Chemotherapy

Chemotherapy is a term used to describe medications that are designed to kill rapidly dividing cancer cells. Many know this type of treatment simply by the word 'chemo', but there are a wide variety of drugs that are used, not just one, as the name implies.

How does it work?

Chemotherapy drugs disrupt the cell division process and kill off the cancer cells by damaging the part of the control centre inside each cell that makes cells divide. Alternatively, it may interrupt the chemical processes involved in cell division.

Matching the type of chemotherapy with the type of cancer and other factors, such as age, is done by an oncologist, a doctor that specialises in cancer treatment. If a child is involved, a paediatric oncologist, a doctor who works with children and childhood cancers, may be in charge of the treatment process.

How the treatment is given

Just as there are many types of drugs used in chemotherapy, there are also different ways to administer the medications. One common way is by intravenous (IV). This means that a small tube is inserted into a vein in the patient and the liquid medication is administered usually from a bag that hangs close to the person receiving it. In this way the medication can go immediately into the patient's bloodstream. Since blood flows throughout the body, it is then able to locate and treat the cancer cells wherever they may be.

If IV medication needs to be given for a prolonged length of time, a permanent IV or a catheter may be inserted into a larger vein, possibly in the chest. These types of IV can prove to be less painful for the patient because there are fewer needles needed to administer the medicines. Even though it seems unlikely, it can actually be more comfortable for a child as well, because it can be easier to play and move around without an IV in the arm or hand.

Other methods of delivering chemotherapy can be by injection into a muscle or skin or perhaps even the spinal fluid. Sometimes an oral medication, a pill or a capsule, may be given with the IV drugs or by itself. Your child's oncologist will explain the different types of medication needed to treat the disease when it is necessary.

Radiotherapy

Radiotherapy is another commonly heard phrase when people describe cancer treatment, but what is it exactly? It is another way to target the cancer cells that are growing in the body. It is different to chemotherapy because it uses high-energy radiation, like X-rays or other particle or proton beams, instead of medication. Radiation used for cancer treatment is different to the kind of radiation used in X-rays to, say, check for a broken bone, or at the dentist.

While radiation can be more localised than chemotherapy, it still affects the healthy cells as well as the cancerous ones. Generally, patients, especially children, tolerate and recover from radiation well, but the doctor and/or treatment team will monitor your child as they go through the treatment.

How does it work

Radiation therapy, or radiotherapy, uses high-energy radiation to kill the cancer cells by damaging their DNA. Once this happens the cells stop dividing or die, bringing a halt to the cell division process.

How the treatment is given

Radiotherapy is delivered at the radiotherapy department in hospital. Usually these rooms are dimly lit and the machines might look quite large or intimidating to a child. The radiation doesn't hurt and it actually only takes a few minutes to do the treatment. The hardest part for your child might be keeping still in a potentially awkward position while the treatment is given.

As with chemotherapy, other cancers, besides leukaemia, are also treated with radiotherapy.

Combination therapies

Many times treatment can be a combination effort. One of the most familiar combination therapies is chemotherapy and radiotherapy together, but there are others that are combined, too. As new medicines become available, new combinations can be implemented. By using more than one treatment at a time, the likelihood of drug resistance may be lessened and it also targets the cancer on many fronts, making the cancer more curable. This multiple treatment approach is used in the treatment of children. Children often hold the most promise for being cured, so using every possible method to treat a child is naturally considered.

'Just as every person is unique or different, so is the way their cancer is treated.'

Other treatment options

Just as every person is unique or different, so is the way their cancer is treated. Combinations ranging from surgery to chemotherapy, radiation and single treatment options are evaluated by doctors in order to tailor the treatment for the best results possible for each individual patient.

For leukaemia treatment some of these other options may be suggested, as well:

▧ A biological therapy – Natural substances are used to stimulate the patient's body into attacking or controlling the growth of the cancer cells. Biological therapy can assist the immune system with recognising and fighting off the cancerous cells, as well as boosting the immune system. Sometimes these medications can even be high doses of vitamins that work more naturally with your body.

- A targeted therapy – A targeted therapy which works on a specific part of a cancer cell, can also be used. For example, chronic myelogenous leukaemia cells contain a protein that a targeted therapy can be designed to break down or to alter in some way. In this way, the drug can work to control the disease's progression, one cell at a time.

- A bone marrow transplant – This procedure, more commonly known as a stem cell transplant, replaces the bone marrow of a person with leukaemia with healthy bone marrow. Bone marrow is where your blood cells are produced so it is where the leukaemia can be targeted. Before the transplant, chemotherapy and radiation therapy are administered in high doses to kill the diseased bone marrow. Your child will need to stay in a special room that is sterile and clear of germs because the chemotherapy and radiation therapy make them more susceptible to infections. Then your child will receive an IV of stem cells, the ones that are used in the bone marrow to create healthy blood cells. These cells work to rebuild the bone marrow in a healthy way and hopefully send the leukaemia into remission.

- Monoclonal antibodies – This treatment involves manufacturing antibodies in a laboratory which are used to target specific leukaemia cells.

Side effects of treatment

Side effects are a concern when beginning any course of treatment. The doctor should explain the expected or most common effects of any course of treatment, so you can help your child understand how they might feel during the process.

While the doctor can explain how some people react to the treatment that your child will receive, the truth is that every person reacts differently and may or may not have the symptoms that are described. There may be medicines or other steps suggested to help alleviate the more uncomfortable side effects.

Side effects of chemotherapy

When chemotherapy is administered, nausea, vomiting, diarrhoea and hair loss may be the most well-known side effects, but other things like mouth sores and a lower resistance to infection may be possible. Extreme fatiguo or tiredness are also to be expected.

Chemotherapy is usually given on a cycle of active treatment and then a rest period with no drugs. These rest times where no medication is administered are called 'recovery periods'. Very often the side effects are lessened or go away completely during recovery periods.

While adults may experience infertility from treatment, children who are treated for leukaemia may or may not have fertility issues when they grow up. Depending on the age of your child, it may be appropriate to ask about freezing embryos or sperm prior to treatment, if there is a possibility of infertility resulting from treatment. A preteen or teenager with leukaemia would most likely be the age group to have that conversation with, since a younger child has many years to fully recover from the treatments before considering having children of their own.

Side effects of radiotherapy

Radiotherapy may make the patient quite tired, so rest is important, but playtime and activity is of equal importance to children, too. Judging how your child feels will help you to create a good balance for them. Keeping them active may also serve them well emotionally, since it feels more 'normal' to play and move around.

Radiation may be directed or focused on a certain point, such as the head for example. In this area, there may be some redness, and itchy, dry skin patches may appear. Some people may experience nausea and a loss of appetite with radiotherapy, but most of the side effects are temporary and can be handled with medications while the treatment takes place.

Side effects of other treatments

Bone marrow transplant side effects can also vary. Since the patient has large doses of chemotherapy and radiotherapy with the transplant, there are increased risks of contracting infections and bleeding more, as well as some of the side effects associated with these two forms of treatment, like nausea, diarrhoea and vomiting. In addition, there can be a systemic reaction to the bone marrow itself. If the bone marrow comes from another person and not the patient themselves, the body can react to the transplanted cells. This can affect organs like the liver and the skin. Treatment with steroids is common to ward off the symptoms of graph versus host disease. The reactions may occur immediately or may happen years later.

Side effects at a quick glance

- Chemotherapy – Nausea, vomiting, diarrhoea, hair loss, fatigue, mouth sores, anaemia and/or bleeding, infertility.
- Radiotherapy – Fatigue, loss of appetite, nausea, red and itchy patches of skin where the radiation is directed.
- Bone marrow transplant – Chemotherapy side effects initially, prone to infections, fatigue, problems with organs and skin rashes if there is a reaction to the transplant, weight gain from steroids.

Again, these are common side effects, but your child may experience some or none, and in varying degrees throughout the course of treatment. Remember, these are a possibility and not a definite occurrence.

Weathering the worst, preparing for the best

With most cancers, a rating system of how much the disease has progressed is used, known as 'staging'. Is the cancer in one place or has it spread to other organs in the body (metastasised)? Is there a tumor? If so, what size is it? These and other questions are posed to help stage or rate the cancer. The stage depends somewhat on those answers. But since leukaemia is a disease of the blood, it is systemic, which means that it could involve all the organs of the body. So therefore, staging is not helpful because leukaemia doesn't follow the same pattern as other cancers.

Instead, leukaemia is described in phases. Some types of leukaemia may have some variation, but generally there are three phases used to label the disease.

Leukaemia phases

* The first is called the chronic phase – This is when there are fewer than five percent of cancer cells in the blood and bone marrow samples. Usually, there are fewer symptoms during this phase and there is a good response to treatments.

* The second is the accelerated phase – When this phase occurs, there is more than the five percent of cancerous cells present in the samples taken and the patient may not respond as well to the typical treatments. A patient in this second or accelerated phase may experience weight loss and/or nausea as well as feeling tired.

* The third phase is called the acute blast phase – In this phase there is more than thirty percent of cancer cells present in the samples and the cancer has spread to other organs. It is a highly aggressive form of leukaemia.

Survival rates

As with any cancer, one of the most important things most people want to know is what the survival rate is with a leukaemia diagnosis. The answer to this is like so many other aspects of cancer diagnosis and treatment: it can be different for each person. However, there are some educated guesses about survival rates that will be based upon the response of other patients your child's age and with their type of leukaemia and the results of their treatment. While the survival estimate is based on many factors, there are new advances every day and so the survival rate is getting better in general.

Survival rates are generally discussed in a five-year period of time. This may be because people who are in remission (see below) are still tracked, and five years is considered a positive length of time to be without any cancer relapse.

Remission

The main goal and priority for all is to achieve 'remission'. Being in remission means that there is no evidence of the cancer following treatment. Understandably, a complete cure is an even more desirable goal, but unfortunately in some cases cancer returns some months or years later, leaving the patient and their family bewildered and devastated if they were told they'd been 'cured'. This is why doctors are often reluctant to use the term 'cured', instead describing the patient as 'being in remission'.

Sometimes, even if no cancer cells are present in the blood tests, a maintenance treatment plan might be made. This provides a lower dose of chemotherapy to make sure that any remaining or stray cancer cells can be killed before they can cause any relapse. The doctor should give you some idea about the survival and remission rates that may be expected for your child. It can then be your decision about how much information to share with them.

'The main goal and priority for all is to achieve "remission".'

What you should know

As with any medical treatment, you should make sure that you ask questions that help you to understand what will happen during procedures, treatment and recovery so that you can help your child understand what to expect.

Before having a test done, you should understand what to do before the test, like whether your child is allowed to eat prior to it or not. Find out where the test is to be carried out and how early you'll need to arrive. Also, how will your child feel after the test? Can he or she go straight home? Do they need to rest for a while? Is there a special way to care for them when you do take them home?

Some treatments may make your child more prone to catching colds and infections. You may have to limit the amount of time they spend with crowds of people in order to keep them as well as possible. Your doctor or treatment team will help you to know when your child can be exposed again.

Since leukaemia is a cancer of the blood, bleeding more than usual, anaemia and fatigue may be things to watch out for during and after treatment. Blood transfusions give healthier blood to a person by IV and one or more transfusions may be needed to help with the anaemia. Usually patients feel much better following a transfusion.

Make sure to tell the dentist about the treatments so they can advise you regarding dental work.

Do not hesitate to ask the questions that help you to feel as comfortable as possible with the procedures. After all, you are an important part of the team because you are the primary support system for your child and you know him/her the best.

'Do not hesitate to ask the questions that help you to feel as comfortable as possible with the procedures.'

Summing Up

- Different symptoms help doctors choose which tests will be more appropriate to form a diagnosis.

- Family history and a full description of all symptoms are usually required from your doctor.

- Doing a blood test is usually the first test performed, as it allows analysis of blood cells to determine if leukaemia is a possibility.

- Other tests involved in diagnosing leukaemia are bone marrow biopsies, lumbar punctures and chest X-rays. Your child may not necessarily undergo all of those.

- Chemotherapy and radiotherapy are common treatments for leukaemia.

- Other treatments that doctors may consider may include a biological therapy, a targeted therapy and a stem cell transplant.

- Common side effects from treatments include nausea, vomiting, fatigue, loss of appetite, skin rashes and more.

- Leukaemia is rated by a series of phases: the first is called the chronic phase, second the accelerated phase, and third, and most aggressive, the acute blast phase.

- There is not a definitive or exact survivial rate for any form of leukaemia. As with most other aspects of cancer and cancer treatment it can be different for each patient, and affected by a number of factors.

- It is essential to be prepared for the fight against cancer by knowing what to expect during procedures and treatments, and all possible outcomes, including the best and the worst.

Chapter Four

Dealing With Effects on Family Life

When there is a diagnosis of leukaemia, life is altered in many ways. The physical changes are not the only ramifications of diagnosis and treatment. There are emotional and financial aspects to consider, as well as the family and school routines become anything but routine.

Preserving 'normal'

Many people ask the question, 'What is normal anyway?' as a matter of conversation or in connection with everyday activities and situations. But, when cancer strikes that question takes on a whole new meaning because in fact, the 'normal' that your family enjoyed, whatever the definition of that was, is now changed in many ways.

An important part of dealing with all of the treatment and the waiting that is often involved, is to establish as much of the 'normal' back into your routines as possible. Also, as treatment ends, returning to the normalilty of life prior to the start of treatment holds challenges of its own.

Some ways to help your child and the rest of the family with getting back to normal may be as easy as establishing a routine bedtime once again. If there are siblings in the home, they may appreciate the 'fairness' of having the sibling who is ill going to sleep at the same time or even earlier than they do.

School may or may not be possible right away; but when it is appropriate, school, and even homework, goes a long way to creating a normal routine like that of well children. You may need to assist your child, the class and the teacher with the re-entry process, but undoubtedly, friends will be a welcomed sight.

If your child is well enough to have visitors, having a play date, even for a short time, would be a welcome activity. If he or she cannot have visitors in person, perhaps consider Skype or FaceTime or even arrange a phone call to make the contact for your child.

Once the schedule returns to something like it was, then you may notice that your child is 'processing' the whole situation. There can be fear and anxiety associated with getting back into the routines of life since the hospital and medical world is so much different. Assisting your child and their siblings with any feelings of anger, sadness or even guilt, is necessary, as well. Talking to you, a counsellor or their doctor may help if these feelings surface in your child or their siblings.

'Only you know what the "normal" was and how best to create what could be your "new normal".'

While your child may appear to be moving along, there can be clues that some worries are lurking. They may begin to show such things as differences in sleep patterns, irritability or tantrums, or even just spending a bit too much time alone. You know your child the best and can start to talk about what might be bothering them if you see some changes.

Only you know what the 'normal' was and how best to create what could be your 'new normal'.

Caring for yourself, so you can care for others

Taking care of your sick child, any other children, a spouse, whilst perhaps still working and overseeing the general running of your household can be a monumental task. If you allow yourself to get too tired and run down, then the emotional battle may seem harder to fight, in addition to the physical illnesses that you open yourself up to by not taking proper care of yourself. What good are you to anyone if you are sick in your own bed and unable be around your poorly child?

Getting rest and recharging your batteries as well as giving in to the emotions that are stored inside, is crucial for you to remain healthy. Having an outlet for your pent-up emotions helps to relieve some of the stress that you feel. Being brave can be a full-time job, but no one works all the time. For you to continue to do everything you need to, you have to be healthy.

Here are some simple tips for you to consider incorporating into your routines:

- Take breaks away from your child – Allow yourself time to nap or chat with a friend or take a walk. Be by yourself or with others, but the time away from your child can help you feel more refreshed. It can allow others to help you in some way by taking care of your child, and in turn your child has an opportunity to be with someone other than you for a bit. It may seem selfish, in fact it is anything but because you are helping to keep the invaluable 'you' available.

- Schedule a date night – Time for you and your spouse or significant other could be a great way to maintain some balance while the treatment is happening. Many couples attempt to schedule one every so often especially when the children are young, but the practice may fade away. If it has faded for you, or if you have not considered it before, perhaps try a meal out or even a movie. Being in public, and not in a hospital, is a healthy way to remind yourself about the world that is still there for you when you are ready to jump back into it.

- Get exercise – It can help clear the mind as well as refresh the body. Whether it is a walk with someone or by yourself, an exercise class or treadmill in the garage, the physical outlet can stretch tired muscles so that they unknot, clear your head of those racing thoughts and help you to remember to breathe.

- Eat right – Make sure you have time to eat. If you are in a rush and are not able to be home for a good meal, carry nutritional snacks with you. Make some complete meals ahead of time so you will only have to defrost, heat and eat on those nights when you are running late or are just too tired to think about making anything. If you have an older child, this may be a great job for him/her to do to help out. Also, during this time, people will offer to help in many different and useful ways. Cooking and delivering hot meals is a great way for others to lend a hand and to feel useful in the process. Let them bring food to your house so you don't have to plan for that meal.

'Being brave can be a full-time job, but no one works all the time. For you to continue to do everything you need to, you have to be healthy.'

Sometimes there may even be a very willing friend who will organise a week of meals or more for you and all you have to remember is when the doorbell chimes, it is dinnertime.

Helpful suggestions

There can be a great deal to keep track of with the testing, getting a diagnosis then beginning the treatment regimen, plus coping with the impact all this has on family life. It is important to feel as involved and in control as possible. Here are some tips to attempt to do just that.

* Ask questions so you understand what the medical terminology means and ensure each procedure is explained.

* Make notes about things you want to know before you get to talk with the doctor.

* Access the services that are available as you need them.

* Keep a list or journal about symptoms or concerns that you have; a personal diary may help you express your feelings i.e. fears and concerns if you aren't able to talk to anybody.

* Attempt to keep your child from getting infections: limit trips out in public.

* Laugh.

* Get plenty of rest where possible.

* Play with your children.

* Eat healthily as often as possible to keep your strength up.

* Talk with someone or tell others how you are feeling if you can.

* Assist your child in describing how they are feeling, both physically and emotionally.

* Accept help from others.

* Join a support group.

* Pray, if this is something you draw strength from.

* Help your children with homework.

- Read a story to the kids.

- Read a book or do something just for you.

- Make meals and freeze them ahead of time.

- Seek financial help, if needed.

- Contact the Leukaemia Society and other organisations for resources and support. (See the help list).

- Keep as many normal things in your family's life as possible, like music lessons or sports for the well siblings.

- Continue to keep hope alive.

Support systems

While navigating through all of the medical language, paperwork and procedures, there are many things to consider. Finding support systems is one of the key ingredients to remaining in control of the difficult situation your family is in. Whether it is a shoulder to cry on, a hand to hold, or assistance with filling out the latest form, it helps to know that there are places to turn.

The following list gives options to consider if seeking support. There are no rules about which or how many resources you access. It is a personal and family decision. You may decide to take advantage of something and as the treatment goes on, you may give something else a try.

- Doctors, nurses and other members of your treatment team.

- Psychologist, psychiatrist or social worker.

- Family and friends.

- Other patients and families in similar circumstances.

- Support groups.

- Respite childcare agencies.

'Finding support systems is one of the key ingredients to remaining in control of the difficult situation your family is in.'

Whatever you choose to do to help your child and your family cope with the situation is up to you. All of the support systems are designed to make it possible for you to hope for the best in the future and to persevere in the present.

'Hope of improvement is the motivation behind accepting every dose of medication prescribed'. Anonymous physician.

Time and money

From diagnosis through to treatment and beyond, there can be several months, or even years, involved in the fight against leukaemia. During this process a huge amount of time is spent at the hospital whilst the patient undergoes tests and treatment, and the family meet doctors and specialists to discuss diagnosis, treatment and progress. Understandably, everyday life is disrupted and time spent travelling, visiting hospital, and coping, pushes out the normal routines.

Living in the UK, we are fortunate to have the NHS to provide our medical treatment and care, meaning parents of children diagnosed with leukaemia do not need to worry about funding the treatment for the cancer. Despite this, there are other financial implications a diagnosis of leukaemia can have on family life. Parents may face the decision that one of them must give up work in order to care for the ill child, and accommodate the new demands placed on the family routine. Obviously, the loss of a regular income will have a huge impact on finances and resources; and this, coupled with the devastating news of the diagnosis, can often be almost too much to bear.

For families already struggling to cope financially whilst their child fights the disease, and for those about to face the fight who are wondering how they will manage as and when one parent leaves work to become the main caregiver, there are some invaluable sources of support that can be accessed.

Visit the Children's Cancer Recovery Foundation website at www.childrenscancerrecovery.org.uk which offers practical support, advice and comfort to families with children affected by cancer. It gives details on how the organisation can help with financial support and advice, as well as the emotional support they offer to the children and families, doing what they can to help them forget the illness where possible by providing rewards for bravery to the child undergoing treatment and opportunities for them to develop and learn whilst fighting the disease.

Something else worth knowing about is the Equality Act 2010, a law which protects people affected by cancer and other serious diseases from discrimination. In accordance with the Act, cancer is considered a disability. In the case of childhood cancer, children's parents are provided the same rights, meaning employers are required by law to make reasonable arrangements with regards to working hours, time off, etc. So, for example, your employer is not allowed to force you to take unpaid leave when you attend hospital appointments with your child. See the help list for more details.

More useful information about the financial implications of leaving work to care for someone can be found at www.macmillan.org.uk/Cancerinformation/Ifsomeoneelsehascancer/Workingwhilecaringforsomeone/Givingupwork.aspx and also www.direct.gov.uk/en/CaringForSomeone/CarersAnd Employment/DG_10027542. See the help list for full contact details.

To find details of any extra financial help or benefits you may be entitled to if giving up work or forced to reduce your working hours, contact the Tax Credit Helpline and Tax Credit Office on 0345 300 3900 or www.direct.gov.uk/taxcredits.

Summing Up

- Leukaemia will affect your family life in many ways, both emotionally and financially.

- Try to keep your family's life as normal as possible, such as arranging school and homework, organising play dates and more.

- Use all resources made available to you.

- Do not be afraid to ask for help whenever needed.

Chapter Five

The First Year
and Beyond

What does the first year hold for your child? Is there much pain involved? How can you help them cope through it all? What challenges will you, your child and the rest of your family face? These and other issues will be addressed in this chapter, to help you and your child understand and overcome what they will face in the first year fighting the disease.

Hills and hurdles

Children who are diagnosed with leukaemia must conquer and manage things that other children their age do not. Sometimes these are emotional challenges that can be addressed right away and/or on a continuous basis as reassurance is needed. In addition to your child who is ill, family members are also digesting the diagnosis and reacting to the information, so assisting them with their emotional responses may also be necessary. When it comes to treatment, there is a cyclical rhythm to it and in some ways learning to deal with leukaemia during the first year and beyond can be cyclical as well. Your child may be feeling okay during one stage, and the fear and anxiety is kept at bay, but by contrast, should they be sick from treatment and in need of extended hospitals stays then their emotions can be very different. So there will be ups and downs, some good days and some not so good ones to expect.

'When it comes to treatment, there is a cyclical rhythm to it and in some ways learning to deal with leukaemia during the first year and beyond can be cyclical as well.'

Facing fear

As parents we believe it is our job, naturally, to allay the fears of our children and shield them from harm, both physical and emotional. Watching your child battling leukaemia, it is easy to put 100% of your emotional resources into reassuring and protecting them from their worries and fears, and subsequently ignoring your own. However this could do more harm than good in the long run. In order for you to be the vital source of support and strength they need, you must address your own fears and concerns so you can help them through theirs. The best ways to do this are by ensuring you stay fully informed every step of the way with what is happening and why, and also by sharing your own emotional burden with those closest to you and the professionals trained to help you. Children look to their parents for answers and help in understanding things, and by staying informed by the doctors and specialists involved in your child's case and accessing the emotional support from nurses, counsellors, friends and family you will be able to answer their questions with courage and conviction, helping to reassure them. Children's reactions often mirror their parents', and if you appear unsure, frightened and confused this will only heighten their anxiety during this uncertain and difficult time.

If you want to reach out elsewhere for support, Macmillan Cancer Support www.macmillan.org, is a great resource for parents and there are many online forums where you can chat to and hear from people who have gone through or are going through the same as you.

Communication

Communication is critical for all concerned, not just the child who is the patient, but you may be the role model of how to communicate your emotions and fears in a way that allows others to express themselves.

Emotions run the gauntlet when dealing with a leukaemia diagnosis. Parents, siblings and the child who is ill all have emotional reactions and may all express them at different times and in different ways. It is important to make sure everyone in the family is able to express themselves as needed. Some behaviours and emotional reactions are also connected to the length and intensity of the medical procesures. Longer treatments or many quick trips to the hospital for intense treatments may invoke very different reactions.

Exposure

The poorly child may not be the only one who'll need your help facing their fears and understanding their emotions. If there are other children in the family or close friends, ensuring that they understand that they can not 'catch' leukaemia from the sick child can be important. Sometimes kids feel that way and don't speak up about it, hiding their worries or misguided beliefs. Explaining to the children directly this is not the case is both helpful for the family unit and also for the friends of the ill child, who will have questions, too. Just talking about it can help all the children connected to the ill child understand and lessen their fear of being with your child even after treatment is completed. The last thing the patient wants on top of everything else is to feel ostracised from brothers or sisters and friends. As mentioned in chapter 4, preserving 'normal' is an important way of helping your child cope through the illness, and being around siblings and friends, to play and chat with is a big part of that.

Physical and behavioural changes in the patient

Losing hair is a side effect from chemotherapy. This is one of the most obvious physical changes from the treatment. Your child may opt to wear a scarf, a hat or perhaps will not cover their head at all. Some children or teens may even want to be fitted for a wig. In any case, the loss of hair will have a huge emotional impact on your child.

There might be bouts of vomiting and diarrhoea and even spiking high fevers that will require attention, as well. Brothers and sisters should be told about what might occur so they are as prepared as possible for these episodes.

Behavioural changes for the sick child and/or from the well siblings can present themselves as life continues during treatment. This can be an emotionally challenging time for all involved. If your child goes through a difficult patch, then their siblings may be more prone to emotional outbursts or perhaps will just be tired due to sleep disturbances and routine upheaval. Your poorly child may understandably be more sensitive or 'touchier' than normal and this may cause some disagreements with siblings or friends.

'Behavioural changes for the sick child and/or from the well siblings can present themselves as life continues during treatment.'

Some patients complain about headaches and may even become more aggressive at school or in public. As a family it will be important to monitor the changes in all of your children because each may be in need of some extra attention, support and love to continue to handle the stress that the leukaemia brings. Sometimes, conversations with counsellors and teachers might be in order to help everyone be involved in a positive and constructive manner.

Gains and losses

Hair loss, again, is one side effect that is feared, but nevertheless expected, in cancer treatment. The type of medications used and the dosages can affect hair loss. Since chemotherapy is designed to kill the rapidly growing cells, the cells in the root of the hairs are affected, as well. The good news is that three to ten months after chemotherapy ends, hair should grow back again.

Weight loss and gain can also occur during treatment. During treatment, the appetite may be diminished and foods may not taste quite the same. This may be quite alarming and offputting for children, so if eating is less enjoyable during treatment, it may be hard to entice your child and weight loss is the result.

By contrast, some types of treatment utilise steroids and they can induce weight gain. While this gain most likely will be temporary and fluid based, it may present its own challenges with eating.

Academic loss is another area of concern. Children who are in treatment may miss a great deal of school, but also when they can return there could be a possibility of infection and even some worry about physical things such as the catheter line being knocked or pulled, or building rest time into the day. Children may also exhibit some learning issues that will need to be addressed as they occur. We will discuss returning to school and its implications in the following section.

Communication, again, is the key to making the people who are important in your child's life understand the roller-coaster ride that you are on. The gains and losses are a part of that since they may come and go just as the hills and valleys of emotions will.

Returning to school

School is one of the most normal routines in a child's life. The hope of returning can be a day to look forward to, but it takes planning. In addition to the time away and the physical concerns about returning to school, some learning issues may become apparent due to radiotherapy or other treatments. Attention issues and trouble processing may be among the challenges. Dealing with these and accessing help can be the key to keeping self-esteem high and ensuring successful reintegration into school. Contact with the head teacher, nurse, and of course the teachers, is critical to the return process. Sorting out the medical management and outlining the potential difficulties that may arise for your child will help bring the school onboard with you as a part of the team looking to create success and a return to good health for your child.

Here is a checklist that may prove helpful when talking to the school:

- Discuss as much relevant medical information as necessary.

- Discuss any possible accommodations and/or adjustments that may be needed upon re-entry.

- Reinforce the fact that your child is 'ready' to return to school according to the doctors.

- Set up a time to speak to the child's class if appropriate or invited by the school.

- Reassure the teacher and head teacher that they will have your support.

- Discuss any worries about them restarting school.

- Answer and consider any fears and questions from the teacher, head teacher and pupils.

- Plan to have your child gradually begin again and plan the schedule in advance.

- Make sure all the contact information is up to date.

- Ask about homework and other requirements for academic success.

Meetings at the school may need to take place on a regular basis, should you feel that type of contact in your child's best interests. Make sure that if an issue arises you speak to the teacher or head teacher right away to deal with it. As any academic issues come up, ask about interventions like one-to-one tutoring to help with the difficulties. You are your child's advocate and can help them achieve success in school after fighting leukaemia by being supportive and active in making it possible.

As worrying or difficult the return to school may be for you, it's a hugely important and positive step for your child, helping them to regain a sense of 'normal' back in their life. Getting back in the classroom means they've escaped the unfamiliar and frightening world of hospitals, appointments and procedures, and returned to one they recognise of fun, learning and socialising. It reinforces the message to everyone that there is life after cancer and a future for them to invest in. CLIC Sargent has a useful website that both parents and teachers can access entitled 'Talking to primary school children about cancer' and discusses how to talk to children if one of their classmates has the disease. www.clicsargent.org.uk/sites/files/clicsargent/field/field_document/TalkingtoPrimarySchoolChildren.pdf

'As worrying or difficult the return to school may be for you, it's a hugely important and positive step for your child.'

Hope

As human beings, we all need hope. With a diagnosis of cancer the main hope is always for a cure. Hope can be hard to find in the first few days or weeks, but it is important to try and keep it alive as you proceed. Hope for a cure or to go into remission can make all the hardship worth it in the end.

If a cure is not possible, then those hopes for a cure change to attaining the best options in treatment and for a life with limited interference by the cancer.

If there is an incurable cancer diagnosis, then hope can also be found in the final plans for a person, too. Hope for a cure for others and hope that the special mark your child has left on the world will be important to others as well as your family.

Whatever the context, it is important for the child who is ill and also the family and friends who love them that hope is kept alive and well in spite of leukaemia.

Living with leukaemia: People's perceptions and reactions

Keeping hope alive is sometimes a hard task and people's reactions to the cancer can complicate the process. Some may be overly nice trying to be accommodating. Others may be a bit brusque because they don't know what to say or how to act. The people who act the most 'normal' might be the ones to whom you can turn when needed.

Since more adults have cancer than children, the reactions may be based on prior experiences with a loved one who has suffered with cancer and sadly even died from the disease. If they are thinking of that whilst interacting with you or your child, then their behaviour might be unexpectedly inappropriate or may surprise or unintentionally upset you.

Communicating how you and/or your child are feeling may help. Acknowledging that you understand it may be hard for that person to interact with your child based on their experience with cancer can often give that person the ability to let that go and start afresh with your child.

For some, the thought of a child with cancer may be hard for them to imagine. Wanting to spare a child suffering is a natural reaction and when there isn't a way to do that, sadness may overshadow other thoughts about the situation. Being comfortable discussing the treatment and other information can sometimes make the topic a bit easier for people to handle. It may even be okay to ask someone about their feelings should they continue to be awkward around you or your child.

The truth is that anyone who hears that leukaemia is the diagnosis will have a reaction on some level and may need time, like you, to process the idea and to move past the initial emotions attached to the news. Given time, many will come around and may become your best support.

As time moves on

Putting the cancer treatment and all of the side effects behind you and your child is definitely a goal emerging from the treatment treadmill, but there may still be some aspects of treatment that do not go away altogether. At the beginning, awaiting the regrowth of hair may still mean your child stands out as different. They may have to continue to attend medical check-ups and have tests even if they are feeling better. Keeping the lines of communication open with the school and family members about needs as time goes on, is still key to keeping hope alive and creating an unbeatable support system for your child.

Summing Up

- There will be many hills and hurdles to conquer during leukaemia treatment.

- You and your child are dealing with the condition, but you also need to remember that your family members and friends are also digesting the diagnosis and reacting to the situation.

- It is important you address your own emotions and fears before helping your child tackle theirs, and to also stay as informed as possible about their condition. Being calm and confident around them will help them cope, and having the knowledge to answer their questions and concerns will help reassure them.

- Both physical and behavioural changes will present themselves in the patient. Hair loss can have a huge impact, leaving the child feeling self-conscious so they may opt to wear a scarf or a hat. Also behavioural changes in the patient and their well siblings may be noticed as treatment takes its toll.

- Academic loss is also associated with leukaemia treatment, as your child may not be able to pursue schooling at a normal pace. It is important to address this issue by discussing it with school staff to ensure that your child benefits from all the resources offered to him or her.

- The return to school can be one of the biggest worries for parents, but also one of the biggest achievements for the ill child. The fact they have been declared fit and ready to go back to school is a hugely positive step in the road to recovery and realising there's life after cancer. By communicating with the school, the pupils and doctors, the transition back in can be positive and successful.

- You may observe changes in your child's behaviour or personality; while this is entirely normal as your child is faced with a harsh reality, it is also important to try and ease his or her concerns and fears.

- People's reactions to the diagnosis and subsequent treatment may differ depending on if they've had their own experiences with cancer.

- The key to facing and overcoming many of the challenges you'll face in the first year or so following diagnosis is communication. Talk to those affected by the issues and access the resources and sources of support available to you.

Chapter Six

Your Child's Medical Team

The journey leukaemia takes your child on is an often long, and always, physically and emotionally difficult one. From the very beginning, you and your child will be involved with a team of specialists who will liaise with you and plan the treatment they feel will be best for your child and most successful based on their diagnosis and prognosis.

Together, this group of doctors and specialists will form the 'multidisciplinary team' (MDT) who you should become familiar with and who will oversee your child's treatment and care.

Your child's MDT

Your child's MDT will be made up of a number of doctors and other health professionals with expertise in a specific cancer and will be led by a consultant oncologist/haematologist who specialises in the treatment of leukaemia. Their MDT may also include:

- A paediatric surgeon
- A clinical oncologist (chemotherapy and radiotherapy specialist)
- A paediatric oncologist (cancer specialist)
- A nurse specialist
- A paediatric haematologist (specialist in blood disorders)
- A dietitian
- A pharmacist

Health professionals from other areas of medicine, such as psychologists, physiotherapists and occupational therapists may also be included.

The MDT meet regularly to discuss and review newly diagnosed children, treatment plans and options, clinical trials and any cases where the patient may be having problems or require extra support.

Your child's MDT will work closely together, using their expertise to provide the information and support needed to give the best treatment possible to achieve the best outcome.

We will look at the roles of some of the members of your child's MDT in more detail in the rest of this chapter.

'Your child's MDT will work closely together, using their expertise to provide the information and support needed to give the best treatment possible to achieve the best outcome.'

Paediatric oncologist

When you enter the treatment phase following diagnosis, primary care of your child will move away from the doctor/GP you consulted initially and there will be other doctors that you meet. An oncologist is a doctor who specialises in cancer treatment. A paediatric oncologist is the doctor who works with children who have cancer. As already mentioned, your family doctor may not be as visible as you move into the active treatment phase, but rest assured all your child's information will be sent to the paediatric oncologists so that they have all the necessary information about your child.

Nurses

Nurses assist doctors with some treatments and procedures. There are different levels of nursing. If a nurse is a registered nurse, then (s)he has graduated from a university or college with a degree in nursing. Nurses assist doctors in the care of patients, doing paperwork and offering information to patients as well.

Specialist registered nurses administer chemotherapy treatment at hospital and, in some cases, at home.

Some nurses add another licence and become a nurse practitioner. Now they have additional specialisation in an area, such as paediatrics, and can do more of the tasks that a doctor would traditionally do. A nurse practitioner can perform a physical exam, order tests, document a health history and, of course, answer your health-related questions. They can also write prescriptions and treat common childhood diseases. If there is a nurse practitioner in the group, then you may see them at the different appointments that you have. If it seems as though the nurse practitioner is in charge at a particular appointment and writes you a prescription, then they may be. Often doctors will have a nurse practitioner share some of their patient visits since they have the medical knowledge and training. Nurse practitioners will also be in close touch with your doctors, so any medications or other suggestions have most likely been discussed with the team prior to the nurse practitioner passing them on to you and your child.

A registered oncology nurse is a nurse who works primarily with cancer patients and around their treatments.

Clinical oncologists

Clinical oncologists are doctors who specialise in treating cancer with chemotherapy, radiotherapy or other drug treatments. You may also hear the doctor referred to as a radiotherapy doctor or radiologist.

Radiotherapy specialist and radiographer

If your child has radiotherapy as part of their treatment they will be under the care of a radiotherapy specialist who will plan, prescribe and supervise their treatment.

A radiographer operates the machines that deliver the treatment. They are highly skilled and trained, and work closely with the radiotherapy specialist to plan treatment. Usually your child should see the same radiographer throughout their treatment, so they will get to know them. Seeing a familiar face during their radiotherapy should help put them as ease and make treatment easier to manage.

'Clinical oncologists are doctors who specialise in treating cancer with chemotherapy, radiotherapy or other drug treatments.'

Specialists

These are the people who work in one specific area of medicine. They lend their expertise as a member of the treatment team, or may be your primary doctor in the process.

Some of the specialists that your child may encounter we've already covered: paediatric oncologist, a doctor who specialises in childhood cancer; also a radiotherapist; and a registered oncology nurse. You may also meet surgeons, a haematologist and even a dietician along the treatment road.

When you meet a specialist, make sure, as with other aspects of treatment, that you get clarification for you and your child regarding terminology, procedures or side effects. Asking questions is the best way to understand what is to come and how it will affect your child.

Dietician

A dietician is someone who plans meals. They know a great deal about nutrition and how foods can help the body to grow strong and healthy. They can be a resource when and if there are some appetite issues with your child. Suggesting ways of getting healthy foods into your child's diet when they don't feel like eating anything can be an invaluable resource.

Surgeon

A surgeon may be needed in some cases. This person will meet with you prior to a surgery date and will explain the procedures and risks to you. He or she will be the one who will do the operation when the time comes. A tour of the operating theatre might be a possibility for your child prior to the surgery. This might make it easier to handle if your child knows what to expect on the day of surgery.

Haematologist

A haematologist is a specialist doctor who studies blood and blood-related diseases. A paediatric haematologist specialises in treating children who have blood diseases, such as leukaemia. Your child's haematologist will interpret the results of their tests to help with diagnosis and use the results to prescribe a specific type of treatment.

Complementary therapists

Parents want the very best for their children and so when leukaemia is diagnosed it is natural to want to take advantage of anything that can prove helpful for your child. Therapies such as aromatherapy, massage and diet plans with and without multivitamins can be considered as a complement to the other treatments, and in some cases in lieu of them. Music and even play can help a child to feel better during chemotherapy or other treatment. The goal of both traditional medications and complementary therapies is to provide as many ways as possible to make treatment easier, tolerated better or to make your child feel much better. Ask your doctor and treatment team what may make sense for you to incorporate into your child's regimen.

Trust and communication with the medical team

Your child is very important, so accessing the best possible treatment for them is critical to the success of the treatment in the long run. There are many new things to learn as you begin the treatment and so trusting your treatment team is imperative. Once you meet the people who will most often be involved in the direct care of your child, then you can begin to build a relationship with them. You will be able to understand how best to communicate with them and how you wish to have information presented. As you get to know them, you may also appreciate some who have a sense of humour or calming disposition that is especially helpful, perhaps. The treatment team needs to function with good communication and to work in the best interests of the patient – your child. If at

'A haematologist is a specialist doctor who studies blood and blood-related diseases.'

any time during the process you feel lost or unable to get the information that you need, ask for a meeting so that you feel as though your voice is being heard and valued.

This clarification can be important on a number of levels. For you, it is needed to clear your mind or to answer questions about something that hasn't been truly explained. For the treatment team, it can let them know that you are in need of something that they may be overlooking at that particular time and they need to readjust to make things flow better. A meeting can serve to get things back on track.

Even if things are moving along well, it may be a good idea to ask for a meeting every so often just to have all the caregivers in the same room at the same time and all focused on your child.

Since your child will be meeting all the different doctors, nurses and specialists, it may be hard to keep track of who is who. They will all know your child's name, but it may be harder for your child to remember all the people associated with their treatment and care. If it is okay with the doctors, nurses and therapists, you could take pictures for your child to look at and to get to know. You can make it a guessing game if you want. If your child is older, pictures may not be appropriate, but maybe suggest a list or notebook just because it will help to make it seem a more personal and less 'sterile' process if you're all introduced and acquainted.

Consenting to treatment

Before commencing any treatment course, the doctor will explain what it entails and what it aims to achieve. After, depending on your child's age, either you or they will be asked to sign a consent form, giving permission for the treatment to go ahead. At the age of 16, a child is usually allowed to give their own consent to treatment, however the law surrounding children consenting to their own treatment is very complex, so make sure you discuss any concerns you have with the doctor.

Before giving consent, make sure you and your child have been fully informed about and understand:

- The type and extent of the treatment

- The advantages and disadvantages of the treatment
- Any side effects that may result from it
- Any significant risks
- Any other treatment options that may be available

Don't be afraid to ask

If you're unsure about any aspect of the treatment, do not be afraid to ask doctors or specialists to explain again. Cancer treatments can be complicated to understand, and it's not unusual for people to require repeated explanations; hospital staff should always be willing to make time for your questions. Afterall, it's important everyone understands how the treatment may affect the patient.

It's beneficial to have your partner, other family member or a good friend accompany you to discussions relating to your child's treatment. At an emotionally difficult time when your thoughts and attention may be elsewhere, having someone else there who will remember the discussion and offer support will make things easier. It may be useful to write a list of questions or points of reference beforehand to ensure you remember everything you want to ask or discuss.

Take your time

It shouldn't be the case that you have to make a decision when the treatment is first explained. Doctors will understand you will want to make the right choices based on the information they've given you, and that you may need time to process the information. There may be situations or emergencies that mean a decision does have to be made quickly, but generally it's usually possible to be allowed more time to think things over.

'If you're unsure about any aspect of the treatment, do not be afraid to ask doctors or specialists to explain again; hospital staff should always be willing to make time for your questions. Afterall, it's important everyone understands how the treatment may affect the patient.'

Clinical trials

Your child may be offered treatment that's part of a clinical trial. If this is suggested, you'll be given information about it and what it involves. If you agree to go ahead, consent will be needed for the trial as well as the treatment. Clinical trials are discussed in more detail in chapter 8.

Summing Up

- A team of healthcare professionals with expertise in your child's specific illness, known as the multidisciplinary team (MDT) will work together to care for and devise the best treatment plan for your child.

- The MDT may consist of a paediatric oncologist, a clinical oncologist, nurse specialist, haematologist and a dietician. Their individual roles are all different but play an equally important part in providing the best care and treatment for your child's leukaemia.

- You will be asked to give your consent before any treatment or procedure can begin. If the child is over the age of 16 they may be able to give consent themselves.

- Before agreeing to any treatment, ensure you are fully informed and understand what the treatment will involve and how it may affect your child.

Chapter Seven

Preparing Against Relapse

Living with the fear of relapse can to some be just as hard as going through the initial diagnosis and treatment of leukaemia. Although relapse is not inevitable, there is no one thing that can definitely prevent it from occuring, but helping your child to be as healthy as possible following completion of treatment is a good start.

Encouragingly, the probablility of relapse decreases with time, although late relapses do occur.

Proactive steps

First, consider exercising on a regular basis. When trying to match a physical activity, ask some key questions about beginning it, such as: what type of exercise would they like to do? Are there any barriers to participation, like finding the time or physical barriers? Consider scheduling the exercise time on a calendar so it becomes another part of the daily routine.

Next, consider adding a vitamin A supplement, but make sure you discuss it with your treatment team to be sure it can be a helpful addition for your child's specific circumstances. Vitamin A is used by the body to promote proper cell growth. There is some evidence that it can play a key role in making cells grow into mature cells instead of continuing to divide in the early stages of cell division.

'Encouragingly, the probablility of relapse decreases with time, although late relapses do occur.'

Utilising a combination of chemotherapy drugs and vitamin A has boosted the remission rates of some leukaemia to ninety percent with a cure rate of about eighty percent. If there is a high risk of relapse, this regimen of treatment may suggested, but with a strong chemotherapy drug.

Discussing the ways to try to prevent a relapse is another way in which your care team can be of assistance.

Read new research

Genetics is the study of genes and heredity in living organisms. It has recently played a part in new methods of treatment and in how accurate some testing for leukaemia can be. By checking the changes that are present in the chromosomes of a leukaemia patient, doctors can make better decisions about the type and dosage of medications to help treat that person.

New research is happening every day. Advances in medicine help to create new drug therapies, better delivery systems and drugs or other measures that seem to aid in relieving some side effects of treatment. By paying attention to the new research, there may be something that has great potential for your child's cancer, or at the very least hearing about a new break-through, no matter how small, can keep hope alive and feed the belief that something can make a difference for patients fighting cancer of all kinds in addition to leukaemia. You never know when a drug or therapy created for another disease will actually play a role in helping your child's disease.

If you hear about something that may be of use in your child's treatment, consult with your child's care team about it.

Specialist organisations, such as Leukaemia & Lymphoma Research, have very insightful and informative websites with large sections dedicated to the subject of new research into blood cancers. See the help list for details.

Fears of relapse

The reality of relapse can cause emotions to surface at different times. Relapse is a time when the cancer comes back and some of the symptoms may return as well. Often during remission, there will be blood tests and check-ups to make sure that your child is still well. There may be a time when chemotherapy or radiotherapy, or maybe even both, is suggested as a proactive way to keep the cancer from recurring. The doses and length of time of a maintenance treatment will not be the same as in full active cancer treatment. The side effects, therefore, should be lessened as well.

If there is a possibility that relapse will occur, or the patient may face long years of treatment, then the emotional wellbeing of the patient may be in jeopardy. How a mother and/or father reacts and their emotional stability also affects the child's ability to deal with the situation. Seeking support throughout the different phases is a good way to deal with the difficult emotional battles that you, your child and other family members must fight in addition to the physical battles of leukaemia when it comes to facing up to the possibility of relapse.

The truth is that there may be a fear of relapse even if the likelihood is slim. Your family has had to deal with some things that most others will not and that can leave emotional scars and deep-rooted fears for a long time. When a 'routine' doctor appointment comes around, it may bring a bit more anxiety than it would prior to treatment. That reaction can be handled by discussing it with your child and family members and bringing it up with your doctor at the appointment. Imagine the relief when a clean bill of health given.

Thinking about a relapse is not a bad thing, but don't let it be a cloud over the sunny days that you have right now and can expect to have in the future with your well child.

To be . . .

'To be' can mean to live or exist. The following list expresses some 'Bes' that might help deal with the leukaemia and possibility of relapse:

- Be informed about treatment.

- Be sensible about what you can handle.

- Be proactive with ways to stay healthy right now.

- Be aware that you can't control everything.

- Be better at letting go of your fears – think the negative thoughts and then let them go.

- Be aware of your limitations and your breaking point.

'Thinking about a relapse is not a bad thing, but don't let it be a cloud over the sunny days that you have right now and can expect to have in the future with your well child.'

- Be expressive with others about your fears and emotions.

- Be loving.

- Be in the present – enjoy the time right now and try not to let fears and worries make you jump ahead in time.

- Be positive as much as possible.

- Be active – get exercise.

- Be 'me' – get some rest and wind down once in a while and enjoy some 'me' time.

- Be where you are emotionally – if you are depressed, be depressed, if you are happy, be happy.

- Be sensible and ask for help when you need it. Treatment of depression and other troubles is available.

- Be able to say yes to offers of meals and other supportive tasks.

- Be an advocate for your child.

'Be hopeful.'

- Be realistic about support, maybe online support groups are for you if you can't make it to a physical location for a meeting.

- Be silly and have fun.

- Be hopeful.

Beyond fear

How people cope with the fear involved in cancer treatment is personal and can be as different as the expression of cancer itself.

Many people may initially not think about how scared they really are about the future or even the present when they observe their sick child. Kids can show fear in many ways. They can be quiet, they can misbehave, put off going to bed, or even run away and hide. Stomach aches or other general ill feeling can also be a sign that fear is present, but how do you pinpoint whether there is fear or side effects? Depending on the age, there are different reactions.

Religion, for some people, can be helpful during stressful times. For others their religious beliefs may be challenged by the onset of cancer. Vicars are always available for counsel and support. Generally, the hospital can put you in touch with an appropriate person for your needs, should you not have anyone on your own.

For some, being spiritual is not dependent on an organised religion or a religious affiliation. Being quiet outside in the sun or meditating can achieve some peace for people, and that may be sufficient.

The key is for all involved to manage the fear so it doesn't become a paralysing emotion. Your child may have a different set of fears than you do, but every fear is real to the person who has it. Being open about your fear and sharing that it won't stop your life or change the way you do things, in fact it may help your child to see that fear is normal and can be managed. Talking about the whole process can be helpful for your family so that the children and adults alike can feel able to express their wealth of emotions, including sadness and fear.

The search for answers, meaning and peace is not easy no matter what method you use – a religious or a spiritual one. But whatever the method, this can be a vital part of your healing process.

Summing Up

▪ Relapse is unfortunately a reality of any cancer. While thinking about relapse is not necessarily a bad thing, it is important to not let it take over your optimism.

▪ Preparing for relapse is the best way to evaluate all possibilities.

▪ Exercising and taking vitamin A supplements can help maintain a good health level and boost remission rates of certain types of leukaemia.

▪ Staying afloat of all the new research constantly under way in relation to leukaemia is also a great way to stay informed and make sure that you are up to date on all new developments, which can come in handy should there be a relapse or a few bad moments.

▪ The most important part of relapse is how you react to it. Being informed, prepared and not letting the relapse define who you are and who your child is will be tremendously helpful in healing once again. Being proactive, aware and positive are all very good ways to handle a relapse.

Chapter Eight

Resources

Patient resources

Since the patient is a whole person who has interests and desires, there are some services that may help them express feelings or just assist in weathering the storm of treatment. Enquire with your treatment team as to what services or activities may be available at your hospital or community.

Here is a list of some possible resources:

- Art therapy
- In-home nursing care
- Respite care – babysitting/caregiving for all children
- Dietary support
- Educational support
- Spiritual support
- Mental health services
- Music therapy
- A play therapist or specialist
- Social worker
- Speech pathologist
- Physiotherapist
- Physical therapist
- Therapy animal visits

■ Special activities planned, like visiting sports figures

Family resources

Gathering information about procedures, treatment and recovery makes the family more able to deal with the issues that arise along the way. A family whose child has been diagnosed with any form of cancer is usually given a key worker who acts as the point of contact with the rest of the child's healthcare team. Normally a clinical nurse specialist is appointed the role of the family's key worker, and should be a first port of call for any questions, queries or concerns.

'The healthcare team overseeing your child's treatment should also assess the family's emotional needs. This is called a "holistic needs assessment".'

Asking what services are available to the family is important at the time of diagnosis, since opportunities for counselling or other supports can be put in place at the start of the treatment journey. The healthcare team overseeing your child's treatment should also assess the family's emotional needs. This is called a 'holistic needs assessment', and is repeated at various stages during the treatment process. It can help identify if any extra care and support should be provided and through what resource.

Find out about family support groups and individual counselling. Decide if the meeting times fit into your schedule and discuss the decision to attend or not at your own family meeting. If anyone in your family feels as though they wish to have an individual appointment, find out how to set it up.

Take advantage of special activities that the hospital offers such as theme days or a party of some sort. Having your family interact in a fun manner at the hospital helps to make it feel as though you all are welcomed and are a part of the community at large during such a difficult time.

Even though you may have had a tour of the hospital areas where your child will undergo treatment, try and set up a time for the rest of your family to go and see where it will all be taking place. This may be helpful when your child discusses what happened during radiotherapy or in the playroom because the rest of the family will know where that is and what it looks like.

Another aspect of family resources is the family itself. Allowing extended family or close friends who are practically family to be helpful in the treatment process somehow, is also a valuable resource to count on. Family members like aunts and cousins can hold a special place for the child who is ill. Having them be more involved and of help in some ways can be a great support to you and your child.

Financial resources

The physical and emotional demands of caring for a seriously ill child can have a huge impact on the whole family. For parents, discovering their child has this potentially deadly disease, and watching them battling it through painful and draining treatment can be the hardest thing they've ever had to cope with. To be a constant source of support for the ill child may mean one parent has to give up work temporarily or permanently, or drastically reduce their working hours. Doing this has obvious negative implications for the family's financial wellbeing; leading to increasing levels of stress and fatigue in an already difficult and challenging situation.

To help reduce the financial burden, there are a number of resources families can access for advice and support. Contacting the Benefit Enquiry Line on 0800 882200 or visiting www.direct_gov.uk/En/Di1/Directories/DG_10011165 is a good place to start for those who have been forced to leave work, as they can find out what benefits the family may be entitled to. There are also several amazing charities that work to help ease the financial difficulties many families face throughout their child's treatment. Some provide free accommodation near to the main treatment facility, removing worries about the cost of travel expenses or even having to rent a property near to where treatment takes place; leaving parents free to focus their attentions on the most important concern – their child. For more details on financial resources see chapter 4 and the help list.

Treatment resources

Bone Marrow Registry

One resource that is available to patients is the Bone Marrow Registry. This donor list or registry is a worldwide listing of donors that could be a match for your child. Since there are more diseases than just leukaemia that can be treated with bone marrow transplants, this list is searched by nearly six thousand people daily looking for a life-saving match.

Clinical trials

Another treatment avenue to explore is that of a clinical research trial. These trials are a much needed step in the creation of new medications and drugs because they allow the company to test them on humans in controlled circumstances before they are released and marketed to the public.

A drug that is widely distributed as a method of treatment must be safe for humans. The safety testing or trial is divided into four phases. When you are selected to participate it will be important to understand what a clinical trial is and in what phase you will be involved.

- Phase 1 is usually conducted with only a few volunteers. It is used to determine factors such as the safe dose range, the side effects and how the body copes with the drug. Usually this is done in a hospital so that the participants can be monitored throughout the trial.

- Phase 2 has a larger number of people involved in the trial and it is designed to test how effective the drug will be and if it works well enough to test in a larger Phase 3 trial. Also it aims to discover more about side effects and management of them. This phase aims to determine which types of cancer the drug can treat. Patients need to meet with doctors during the trial to monitor their progress just like in Phase 1. Some participants may be asked to write down their symptoms or other health-related information to be used for the next phase.

- Phase 3 is the time where the drug is tested against the current 'best' drug that treats the illness that the experimental drug is targeting. Usually this time, the drug is given to a much wider group of people. A large report is generated at the end of the Phase 3 trial detailing as much information about the drug as possible. Many times this is the phase where a drug falls out of the running due to the side effects or other issues that become clear with the wider group taking it.

- Phase 4 is the phase that occurs after there is permission for the drug to be sold. It is used to determine the long-term risks and benefits and establish its side effects and safety. If there are any adverse side effects or poor drug interactions at this stage, then the drug could be pulled from the market, immediately.

When deciding to be involved in a clinical trial, make sure you are aware at what stage your child will be participating and what the expected or projected side effects and benefits of being involved can bring. Of course with every trial there is a great deal of hope that rides on its success, so to be a part of that ultimate happy ending would be wonderful. A great deal of information should be given to you and you should weigh up the pros and cons of deciding to take part in a research trial carefully.

Becoming a resource

As your child completes their course of treatment and you move away from the day-to-day connection with the hospital, you may have also reached another milestone in addition to the completion of treatment – you could be a valuable resource for other families who are fighting their own battle with cancer.

Reaching out to others as an advocate for more funding, or additional services can be a fulfilling way to contribute to a worthy cause. Based on personal experience, one that is now near and dear to your heart.

Advocacy is not for everyone, so even if you help out by completing a survey or an interview, your feedback is important information for the caregivers and medical personnel involved in the treatment of leukaemia and other blood cancers.

'With every trial there is a great deal of hope that rides on its success, so to be a part of that ultimate happy ending would be wonderful.'

Other ways of lending support may be to participate in a group discussion with other patients or parents of patients, or joining a committee that is charged with a specific focus or purpose that might only meet for a short time. Speaking at a support group is another means of helping others and giving something back.

Whatever your contribution, the reality is that someone else is now walking in your footsteps. Those who were helpful to you probably proved to be invaluable, so maybe you could return the favour in some small way.

As with all the other points in the journey, this one also presents yet another decision. While it may be a great feeling to help another family as they navigate through their cancer nightmare, you must also know how this assistance can benefit you and your family or child. Perhaps your child could be a positive role model for someone else beginning treatment. For example, assisting another child with learning how to behave and keep still on the table for a radiotherapy session may help your child progress in a positive way.

However, it could also be another stressor for you and your family, so you will need to take time to consider how involved you wish to be as a resource to others.

As with other decisions, there is no real right or wrong in this case. It may be something that you do now but move away from, or just the opposite; you may not participate now but become involved at a later date. Regardless, you will feel great about helping and your service/volunteering will be appreciated whenever you see fit to contribute, so do it when it feels like the right time.

Summing Up

- There are many resources available to patients and their family and it is very important that you take advantage of everything that is being offered.

- For the patient directly, things like educational support, music therapy, physiotherapy and animal therapy can all be tremendously helpful.

- There are a number of professional organisations (charitable and non-charitable) that families can contact for advice on helping improve the financial difficulties they may face. Being relieved of the financial burden is an enormous help as it leaves parents free to focus on the treatment of their ill child, and able to offer full support to them and any other family members that need it.

- For the patient's family, there is the possibility to attend family support groups and individual counselling to help deal with the reality of being close to a leukaemia patient. Families can also take part in special activities organised by hospitals and treatment facilities that are designed to bring friends and family together in a joyful experience while dealing with an extremely difficult one.

- Once you've handled leukaemia – whether as a patient, family member or friend – you can become a resource yourself. Your own experience can serve to help individuals who have recently been diagnosed or live with someone who has been diagnosed. Participating in group discussions can also help you make a valuable contribution in someone else's life.

Glossary

Biopsy

A biopsy is a medical procedure involving the removal of a piece of tissue or specimen, in order to conduct a diagnostic study leading to diagnosis.

Bone marrow

The bone marrow is defined as tissue filling the cavities of the bones. This tissue is soft and fatty, and includes reticular fibres and cells.

Clinical trial

Clinical trials are used to develop data and statistics related to the efficiency of a particular new or improved treatment.

Complementary therapies

Related to alternative medicine, complementary therapies are ways to heal the body without the use of Western medicine. For example, complementary therapies can include aromatherapy, massage therapy, acupuncture and other types of healing methods using a holistic or natural approach to the human body.

Diagnosis

The process in which a doctor or a team of doctors can determine the cause of a set of symptoms; coming to a diagnosis usually entails thorough examination and tests.

Graft versus host disease (GVHD)

GVHD is known to be a complication occurring after a transplant. When GVHD occurs, the new tissue that has been transplanted attacks the recipient's body. This can occur in bone marrow transplants.

Oncologist

A doctor specialised in treating cancer – the science studying cancer is called oncology.

Recovery
Return to a healthy state; the fight against cancer, if successful, results in recovery. The word recovery can also be used to describe the process of getting better and healing.

Remission
A period of time following completion of treatment when there are no signs or symptoms of the disease.

Relapse
When a disease that has been treated comes back, it can be defined as a relapse. The recurrence of cancer is a relapse.

Stem cells
These cells are known to divide into various specialised types of cells, as well as self-renew to produce more stem cells. These cells are generally used in transplants related to leukaemia when there are no matches in the bone marrow donors' database, and can help restore the immune system after chemotherapy or radiotherapy.

Thyroid gland
The thyroid gland is located at the base of the neck and secretes hormones in order to control the metabolism as well as the body's growth.

Transplant
In the medical field, a transplant is the act of taking an organ or tissue from a donor and implanting it in the body of the receiver. For example, leukaemia patients will receive bone marrow and stem cell transplants.

White blood cells
Blood contains various cells, some of which are the white blood cells. These are the ones that protect the body from infection and diseases. They are less numerous than red blood cells and are formed mostly in the bone marrow.

Help List

Cancer Information Resources

Anthony Nolan Donor Registry

Anthony Nolan
2 Heathgate Place
75-87 Agincourt Road
London
NW3 2NU
Helpline: 0303 303 0303
Website: www.anthonynolan.org
This amazing charity save the lives of people with blood cancer who need blood stem cell, bone marrow or cord blood transplants.

Cancer Aid and Listening Line (CALL)

Helpline: 0845 123 2329
Website: www.canceraid.co.uk
Emotional and practical assistance for leukaemia patients in the UK.

CancerHelp UK

Freephone Helpline: 0808 800 4040
Website: www.cancerhelp.cancerresearchuk.org
Providing information and resources for leukaemia patients and their famiiies.

The Children's Cancer and Leukaemia Group (CCLG)

University of Leicester
3rd Floor, Hearts of Oak House
9 Princess Road West
Leics LE1 6TH
Website: www.cclg.org.uk
Email: info@cclg.org.uk

The national professional body responsible for developing and organising children's cancer treatment in the UK, through national and international clinical trails. They also provide information to children and their families about cancer.

Children with Cancer and Leukaemia: Advice and Support for Parents (CCLASP)

Unit 7
North Leigh Sands
Edinburgh EH6 4ER
Website: www.cclasp.net
Email: info@cclasp.net
Tel: 0131 467 7420
Run by parents of children with cancer, this charity provides information and organises fun events. Also it offers a helpline and practical support such as transport to hospital/clinics.

CLIC Sargent

Horatio House
77-85 Fulham Palace Road
London W6 8JA
Website: www.clicsargent.org.uk
Email: info@clicsargent.org.uk
Tel: 0300 330 0803
Provides information and support for young people diagnosed with cancer, and their families.

Christian Lewis Trust Kids Cancer Charity

62 Walter Road
Swansea SA1 4PT
Website: www.christianlewistrust.co.uk
Email: enquiries@christianlewistrust.co.uk
Tel: 01792 480500

Offers telephone support plus a range of other support services to children with cancer, and their families. Bereavement support, self-help parent support groups available. Also crisis breaks to places like Wales and Disneyland Paris, play therapy and holiday programmes are offered.

Cruse Bereavement Care

Tel: 01738 444178
Email: info@crusescotland.org.uk
Website: www.crusebereavementcare.org.uk
This organisation helps with support, counselling and advice through the grieving process.

The Equality Act

www.gov.uk/definition-of-disbility-under-equality-act-2010
Provides details about The Equality Act and how it can protect your rights in the workplace.

Gaps: Line

PO Box 92
Dereham Road
Bawdeswell NR20 4WD
Website: www.gapsline.org.uk
Support line: 0845 121 4277
Gives families and carers of children with cancer the opportunity to talk to trained volunteers who have faced the same difficulties.

Irish Cancer Society

Cancer helpline: 1 800 200 700
Website: www.cancer.ie
Ireland's national cancer charity. Offering support, care, and helping to create awareness. They provide information and fund research.

Leukaemia & Lymphoma Research

Tel: 020 7405 2200
Email: info@beatbloodcancers.org.uk
Website: www.leukaemialymphomaresearch.org.uk

www.beatbloodcancers.org.uk
Leukaemia and Lymphoma Research is the only UK charity solely dedicated to research into blood cancers. It provides free patient information, support and general advice on treatment.

Leukaemia Care

1 Birch Court
Blackpole East
Worcester WR3 8SG
Website: www.leukaemiacare.org.uk
Email: care@leukaemia.org.uk
24 Hour Careline: 08088 101 444
Tel: 01905 755977
Offers a huge range of services to people affected by leukaemia and other blood disorders, including a phone line staffed by volunteers, financial grants and support groups

Little Princess Trust

28 Castle Street
Hereford HR1 2NW
Website: www.littleprincesstrust.org.uk
Email: info@littleprincesstrust.org.uk
Tel: 0845 0942169
The Little Princess Trust supply and fund the cost of wigs designed specifically for children. They provide a personal fitting and styling service to ensure the wig is as close as possible to the original hair.

Macmillan Cancer Support

89 Albert Embankment
London SE1 7UQ
Website: www.macmillan.org.uk
Email: cancerline@macmillan.org.uk
Macmillan CancerLine: 0808 808 0000
This great organisation helps improve the lives of those affected by cancer. As well as medical advice, they provide practical and financial advice and support, and run helplines giving cancer information and benefits advice.

Marie Curie.org

Freephone: 0800 716 146
Website: www.mariecurie.org.uk
Runs a nationwide network of nurses providing free hands-on palliative care in patients' homes.

Sick Children's Trust

Website: www.sickchildrenstrust.org
Email: info@sickchildrenstrust.org
Aims to help seriously ill children and their families by providing support and accommodation during hospital treatment. They currently have eight 'Homes from Home' around the country providing clean and welcoming environments for families affected by childhood cancer.

References

About Kids Health, 25 January, 2010, Sonia Lucchetta, MSW, RSWOussama Abla, MD [online] Available at: http://www.aboutkidshealth.ca/En/ResourceCentres/Leukemia/LivingwithLeukemia/Pages/default.aspx accessed on 19 May, 2012

American Cancer Society [online] Available at: http://www.cancer.org/Cancer/LeukemiainChildren/OverviewGuide/childhood-leukemia-overview-survival-rates accessed on 18 May 2012

Blood and Lymphatic Cancers Leukaemia Care, [online] Available at http://www.leukemiacare.org.uk/ accessed on 20 May, 2012

Canadian Cancer Society [online] Available at http://www.cancer.ca accessed on 18 May 2012

Cancer.net [online] Available at: http://www.cancer.net accessed on 16 May 2012]

Cancer Care [online] Available at: http://www.cancercare.org/publications/87-managing_practical_concerns_raised_by_cml accessed on 18 May 2012.

Cancer Compass, [online] Available at: http://www.cancercompass.com/leukemia-information/side-effects.html accessed on 18 May 2012

Children living with cancer planning and support guide for schools, preschools and childcare services, 2000, Department of Education, Training and Employment [online] Available at: http://www.decd.sa.gov.au/speced2/files/pages/chess/hsp/Pathways/cancerbook.pdf accessed on 19 May, 2012

Children's Cancer and Leukaemia Group, End Of Treatment What Happens Next? [online] Available at: http://www.cclg.org.uk/products_files/CCLG-EndofTreatment_Parents.pdf accessed on 19 May, 2012

Children's Leukaemia Research Project [online] Available at: http://www.clrpireland.com/content/index.php accessed on 4th April 2012

Need - 2 - Know

Available Titles Include ...

Allergies A Parent's Guide
ISBN 978-1-86144-064-8 £8.99

Autism A Parent's Guide
ISBN 978-1-86144-069-3 £8.99

Blood Pressure The Essential Guide
ISBN 978-1-86144-067-9 £8.99

Dyslexia and Other Learning Difficulties
A Parent's Guide ISBN 978-1-86144-042-6 £8.99

Bullying A Parent's Guide
ISBN 978-1-86144-044-0 £8.99

Epilepsy The Essential Guide
ISBN 978-1-86144-063-1 £8.99

Your First Pregnancy The Essential Guide
ISBN 978-1-86144-066-2 £8.99

Gap Years The Essential Guide
ISBN 978-1-86144-079-2 £8.99

Secondary School A Parent's Guide
ISBN 978-1-86144-093-8 £9.99

Primary School A Parent's Guide
ISBN 978-1-86144-088-4 £9.99

Applying to University The Essential Guide
ISBN 978-1-86144-052-5 £8.99

ADHD The Essential Guide
ISBN 978-1-86144-060-0 £8.99

Student Cookbook – Healthy Eating The Essential Guide
ISBN 978-1-86144-069-3 £8.99

Multiple Sclerosis The Essential Guide
ISBN 978-1-86144-086-0 £8.99

Coeliac Disease The Essential Guide
ISBN 978-1-86144-087-7 £9.99

Special Educational Needs A Parent's Guide
ISBN 978-1-86144-116-4 £9.99

The Pill An Essential Guide
ISBN 978-1-86144-058-7 £8.99

University A Survival Guide
ISBN 978-1-86144-072-3 £8.99

View the full range at **www.need2knowbooks.co.uk**.
To order our titles call **01733 898103**, email **sales@
n2kbooks.com** or visit the website. Selected ebooks
available online.

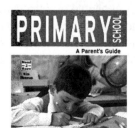
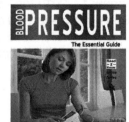
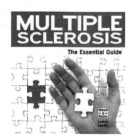

Need - 2 - Know, Remus House, Coltsfoot Drive, Peterborough, PE2 9BF